Real-Life Superpowers

KINDNESS IS A SUPERPOWER

by Mari Schuh

PEBBLE

a capstone imprint

Published by Pebble, an imprint of Capstone
1710 Roe Crest Drive, North Mankato, Minnesota 56003
capstonepub.com

Library of Congress Cataloging-in-Publication Data is available on the Library of Congress website.
ISBN: 9780756574574 (hardcover)
ISBN: 9780756574529 (paperback)
ISBN: 9780756574536 (ebook PDF)

Summary: Every act of kindness counts, no matter how small! Smile at someone in the hallway. Help a neighbor rake leaves. Be a good listener. When you're kind, you make a big difference in the lives of people around you. Show this real-life superpower, and watch kindness spread!

Image Credits
Getty Images: Dobrila Vignjevic, 18, FatCamera, 15, 16, Halfpoint Images, 9, Images By Tang Ming Tung, 11, JGI/Jamie Grill, 10, Jose Luis Pelaez Inc, 7, Klaus Vedfelt, 5, Mike Kemp, 17, pixdeluxe, 19, SolStock, 13; Shutterstock: Kapitosh, design element (background), Mega Pixel, 20, Monkey Business Images, 6, Rosemarie Gearhart, 21, Tatiana Gordievskaia, 12, TinnaPong, cover

Editorial Credits
Editor: Carrie Sheely; Designer: Bobbie Nuytten; Media Researcher: Rebekah Hubstenberger; Production Specialist: Whitney Schaefer

All internet sites appearing in back matter were available and accurate when this book was sent to press.

Table of Contents

Words in **bold** are in the glossary.

Kindness Matters

Think of a time when someone was kind to you. What did they do? How did it make you feel?

We can be kind in the way we think, feel, and act. Kind people care how others are feeling. They try to help them so they feel good. When people are kind, they are caring and helpful. They share with others.

Kindness is a **superpower**. Why? It makes other people happy. Being kind can make you happy too. Kindness helps people in big ways. When people are kind, they help others feel **valued**. Then more people want to be kind to others. Kindness spreads!

Sometimes people forget to be kind. Maybe they are in a hurry. They could be sick or tired. Maybe they are having a bad day.

When people are not kind, they do not think about how others feel. They might think only about themselves. This can make people around them sad, mad, or **nervous**.

Kindness at Home

You can be kind at home in many ways. Did your sister have a bad day? Give her a hug. Is your brother teasing you? Do not get upset. Speak kindly to him.

When it's time to watch TV, let others pick the show. Help others get ready for a meal. At dinner, pour a glass of water for someone.

Being kind takes **practice**. Find new ways to be kind. Rake leaves for a sick neighbor. Did your brother lose his toy? Help him find it. Share your toys. Speak kindly to others, even when they are not kind to you.

Be kind to Earth. Pick up **litter** in the park. Do not waste water.

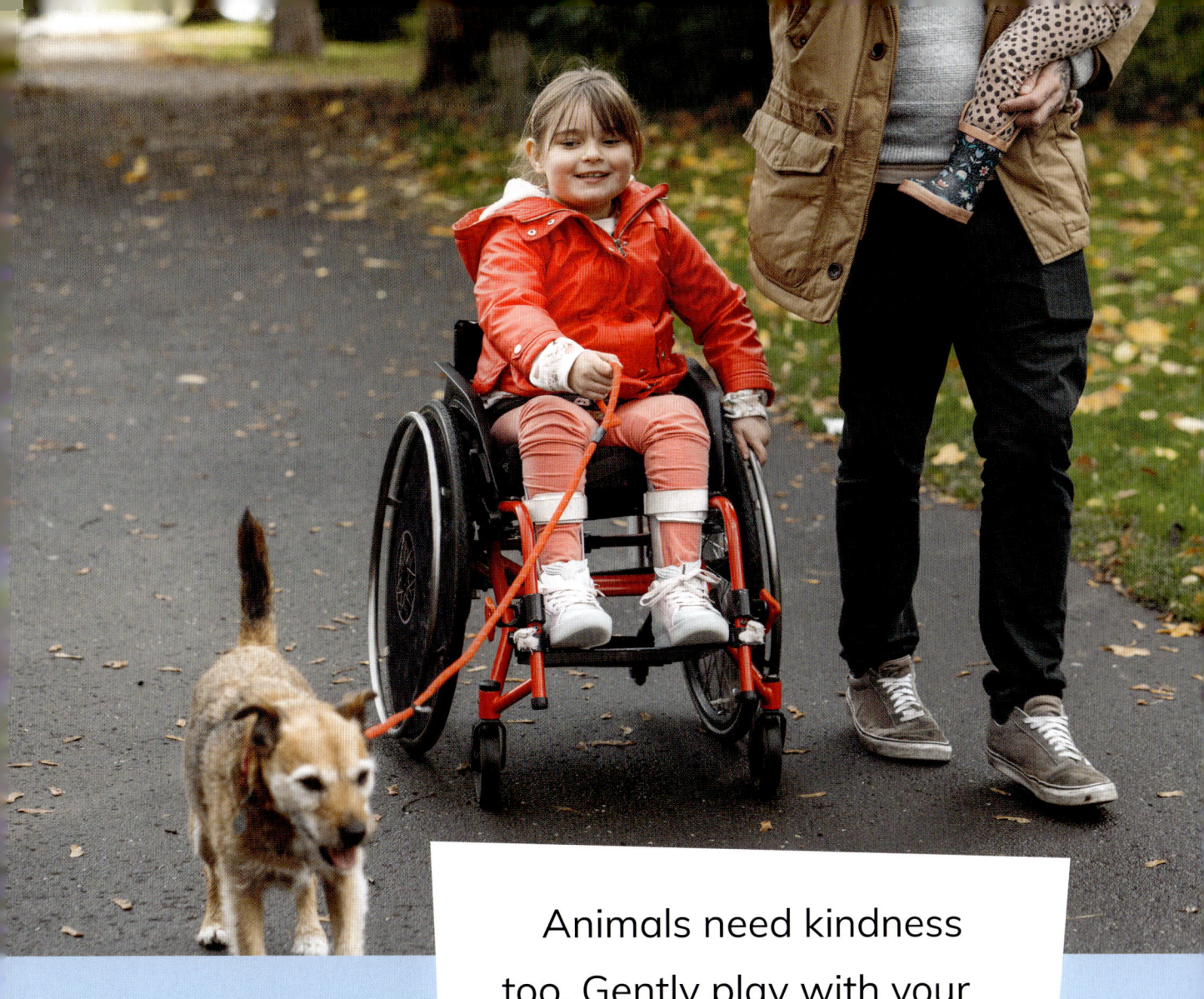

Animals need kindness too. Gently play with your friend's cat. Take your dog for a walk.

Kindness at School

Be kind to others at school every day. If you like their backpack or haircut, let them know. Is a classmate being teased or **bullied**? Speak up for them. When someone drops books, help pick them up.

Do you have new classmates? They might feel nervous or lonely. Eat lunch with them. Ask them to play with you at recess.

When you listen to others, you show kindness. Pay attention to your teachers. If a friend is worried or upset, be a good listener. Let them talk about how they feel. Then ask how you can help.

Smile at everyone you see at school. Thank them when they help you. Make a thank-you note and give it to them. You are spreading kindness!

Be Kind to Yourself

It's also important to be kind to yourself. Think good thoughts about yourself. Always do your best. It's OK if you make a **mistake**. After all, everyone makes mistakes.

Stay active and eat healthy foods. Rest when you are tired. Then you will feel great. It will be easier for you to be kind.

Use your superpower of kindness every day. You will help make the world a happier place!

Kindness Game

People like to hear others say good things about them. Spread kindness with this fun game!

What You Need:

- a soft ball
- a group of friends or family members

What You Do:

1. Gather your friends or family members. Stand in a circle facing one another.

2. Gently toss the ball to one person. Say something kind about that person. Maybe it's something you like about them. Or it could be something they did that makes you proud. Sit down when you are done talking.

3. Now that person tosses the ball to someone else who is standing. They say something kind about them, and then they sit down.

4. Keep going until everyone is sitting down. Kindness has spread around the circle! How does everyone feel?

Glossary

bully (BUL-ee)—to be mean, scare, or pick on someone

litter (LIT-ur)—garbage scattered around carelessly

mistake (muh-STAKE)—something done wrong

nervous (NUR-vuhss)—being worried and uneasy

practice (PRAK-tiss)—to keep working to get better at a skill

superpower (SOO-pur-pow-ur)—an important skill that can affect yourself and others in a big way

valued (VAL-yood)—worthy and important

Read More

Collins, Jordan. *It's Great to Be Kind.* New York: Children's Press, 2021.

Lindeen, Mary. *Being Kind to Animals.* Chicago: Norwood House Press, 2021.

Rossiter, Brienna. *Being Kind to Friends.* Lake Elmo, MN: Focus Readers, 2021.

Internet Sites

BrainPopJr.: Empathy
jr.brainpop.com/health/feelingsandsel/empathy

PBS: Make Your Own Thank You Cards
pbs.org/parents/crafts-and-experiments/make-your-own-thank-you-cards

Wonderopolis: What Is a Random Act of Kindness?
wonderopolis.org/wonder/what-is-a-random-act-of-kindness

Index

About the Author

Mari Schuh's love of reading began with cereal boxes at the kitchen table. Today, she is the author of hundreds of nonfiction books for beginning readers. Mari lives in the Midwest with her husband and their sassy house rabbit. Learn more about her at marischuh.com.